KT-116-660

A GUIDE TO

CHURCH REVITALIZATION

R. ALBERT MOHLER JR, EDITOR

GUIDE BOOK NO.   *oo*5

Table of Contents

CHAPTER 1

CHRIST WILL BUILD AND REBUILD HIS CHURCH:

The Need for 'Generation Replant'

R. ALBERT MOHLER JR.

One stunning building in Manchester, England, is now a climbing center. In Bristol, one is now a circus school, with trapezes hanging from the rafters. Others are now grocery stores, car dealerships, libraries, and pubs. All over England, many are now Islamic mosques.

What do these venerable buildings have in common? Until recently, all formerly housed Church of England congregations. The secularization of Britain is not a new development, with church attendance falling for decades. But a new tipping point has been reached: the Church of England now has an official "Closed Churches Team" that makes decisions about what to do with abandoned church buildings.

Between 1969 and 2011, the Church of England knocked down 500 churches and "deconsecrated" another 1,000. That pace is set to increase dramatically, and England is not alone. The Montreal Gazette recently reported that 340 church buildings are now seeking "new vocations," with that Canadian city now representing one of the most secularized metropolitan areas in North America. Neighbors did not even notice that one Methodist building no longer housed a congregation. They found out when the large stone

Do we have the courage and conviction necessary to replant churches?

building collapsed and no one seemed to care.

The same will soon happen in the United States of America. In downtown Louisville, Kentucky, former church buildings now house doctors' offices and other businesses — but the problem is no longer limited to the inner cities. Churches are closing in the suburbs as well.

According to a report from the Assemblies of God, 4,000 congregations close their doors in the United States every year, while only about

1,000 evangelical churches are planted. We are falling further behind.

Add to this the fact that between 80 and 90 percent of all evangelical churches in the United States are not growing, and a significant percentage are in outright decline. We face a major turning point in the history of evangelical Christianity in America, and the Southern Baptist Convention and its churches are at the center of a great and unavoidable question: "Do we have the courage and conviction necessary to replant churches?"

The idea of church replanting may be new, but this pattern is also as old as the New Testament.

A New Direction

For the past 30 years, evangelicals have been learning anew the importance of church planting. Excitement and passion for church planting come right from the New Testament, which is a manifesto for planting rightly ordered churches. A generation of young evangelical pastors have been righteously infected with the vision for church planting. Their heroes are church planters, their inspiration is church planting, and their missiology is directed toward the birth of new churches. That must continue. Church planting must remain at the forefront of our mission efforts. The only documentable evangelistic and congregational growth experienced by evangelicals within America's major urban areas directly traces back to newly planted churches — and replanted churches.

The idea of church replanting may be new, but this pattern is also as old as the New Testament.

In Revelation 2:1-7, Christ warns the Ephesian church that they have "left [their] first love" and grown spiritually cold and ineffective in ministry. Jesus told the church to "repent and do the deeds [they] did at first."

In other words, that congregation needed a reformation. At some point, declining churches actually need to be replanted.

In one sense, this is just a matter of stewardship. All around us are churches falling into patterns of decline and decay. Most of these churches started with a gospel vision and a "first love" for Christ that propelled them into existence. For some time, most of these churches experienced years of effective ministry, reaching their communities and reaching out to the world. Somehow, at some time, for some reason or combination of reasons, they lost that first love and the ministry was endangered.

Practical realities also play a role in understanding this stewardship. All over New York City, for example, young evangelical church plants are looking for places to meet. A hostile city government threatens to evict all churches from meeting in public school auditoriums and many will be homeless. At the same time, vacant or near-vacant church buildings dot the horizon.

There is also the fact that millions of Christians remain in these declining and decaying congregations. These Christians represent a wealth of experience and an army of workers. In many cases, what they most lack is visionary, courageous, and convictional pastors and leaders.

Then there is this obvious fact: if existing congregations do not thrive, there will be no one to plant, sustain, support, and lead church planting. We cannot have one without the other.

May This Be Our Story

Consider also that many of the most exciting church ministry stories of this generation have come from replanted churches. We can look around the country and quickly find church buildings, once empty, now filled with young families and students, senior adults and business executives.

We need to tell the stories of these churches, even as we continue to tell the stories of

A passion for replanting a church must be matched by skills in ministry and a heart for helping a church to regain a vision.

newly planted churches. Both contexts of ministry require courage. Both require vision and conviction. Neither is the answer

in itself, and both should be celebrated together.

But one of our central tasks in the present generation is to be bold in our vision of replanting churches — helping existing churches to find new vision, new strategic focus, new passion for the gospel, new hunger for the preaching of the Word, new love for their communities, and new excitement about seeing people come to faith in Jesus.

Replanting churches requires both courage and leadership skills. A passion for replanting a church must be matched by skills in ministry and a heart for helping a church to regain a vision. Church replanting and church planting are both frontlines of ministry and mission. And I am excited to see what God will do in this age with a generation of young pastors ready to plant and replant gospel churches with unbridled passion.

Of course, this will also require that churches in decline recognize the need for radical change and reorientation in ministry. No young pastor worthy of his call will be excited to assume the pastorate of a church that simply wants to stem the losses or slow the decline by doing slightly better than the congregation at present. Sadly, many of these churches will die by congregational suicide. Unwilling to be replanted, they simply want a slower decline. This is disobedience to Christ.

Given the scale of our need, this rising generation needs to be known as "Generation Replant." If it is not, it might not be long before the Southern Baptist Convention needs a "Closed Churches Team." May that day never come. Instead, may all of our churches, new and old and in between, follow the promise of 1 Corinthians 3:6 — Paul "planted, Apollos watered, but God gave the growth."

CHAPTER 2

BREATHING NEW LIFE INTO DYING CHURCHES

KEVIN EZELL

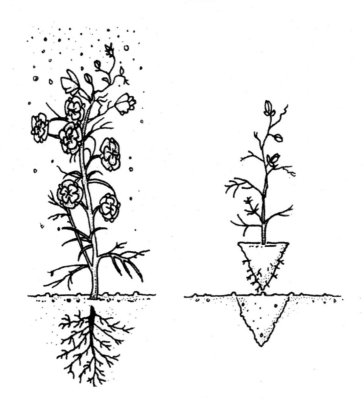

At the North American Mission Board (NAMB), our mission is to help Southern Baptists push back lostness in North America. Our primary strategy for doing that is called Send North America, and that strategy includes two primary goals. First, we want to increase the church birth rate by helping Southern Baptists start 15,000 new churches over a 10-year period. Second, we want to help decrease the church death rate.

The reason both of these endeavors are so important is because Southern Baptists have lost significant ground in the church-to-population ratio during the last 100 years. In 1900, there was one Southern Baptist church for every 3,800 people in North America. Today, that number is one for every 6,200. In the South, that ratio is much better (one SBC church for every 2,722 people). But in other regions, we have much work to do: the ratio is 1:15,885 in the West; it's 1:36,998 in the Northeast, and in Canada it's 1:117,925.

These widening gaps come from two problems: first, we have not started enough churches — especially in and around cities where 83 percent of North Americans live; second, each year an average of 1,000 SBC churches disappear.

Viewed through the lens of any research you look at, Southern Baptist churches are in the midst of a health crisis and have been for many years.

We analyzed data from the Annual Church Profile (ACP) and found that between 2007 and 2012, only 27 percent of reporting SBC churches experienced growth. Forty-three percent

Viewed through the lens of any research you look at, Southern Baptist churches are in the midst of a health crisis and have been for many years.

were plateaued, and 30 percent declined. But our analysis looked at membership numbers. A study by the Leavell Center for Evan-gelism and Church Health at New Orleans Baptist Theological Seminary looked at worship service attendance and found that in 2010 only 6.8 percent of SBC churches were healthy according to that rubric.

These trends should concern everyone. Even if we are successful in starting thousands of new churches over the next few years, if less than 10 percent of established SBC churches are healthy and growing, we cannot hope to keep pace with population growth.

Partnering to Help Churches at Risk

It's not an easy thing to say, but

> It's not an easy thing to say, but some of the churches that die each year need to. They have long since outlived their purpose.

some of the churches that die each year need to. They have long since outlived their purpose. They have been a hollow, ineffective presence in their communities for years. But many more churches have members with a heart for the gospel who want to reach their communities for Christ. They might have lost touch with their communities' new demographics or been derailed by poor leadership. If these churches want to be helped, they can be.

NAMB is trying to solve this crisis in several ways, and many of our state convention partners are also doing very good work, such as:

One-Day Conferences

In 2011, we began partnering with Johnny Hunt, former president of the SBC and pastor of Woodstock First Baptist Church near Atlanta, to conduct a one-day Church Growth and Revitalization Conference for pastors. Johnny has a heart for encouraging pastors, and his church has helped churches in the Atlanta area regain their spiritual footing and become vibrant gospel proclamation centers

> Some churches cannot be redirected toward health without some dramatic changes.

again. Our state convention partners make venue arrangements and we take care of the rest.

Individualized Tools and Resources

After attending our one-day conference, many pastors and churches start to realize they need outside assistance if they are to put their churches back on a path to growth. That is where our state convention partners step in. They are equipped to work closely with individual churches, and we are making funds available for assistance as they help their churches get on the road to health.

Legacy Church Planting

Some churches cannot be redi-

If we don't step in to help these dying churches, over the next few decades we will see thousands of properties worth millions of dollars slip through the hands of Southern Baptists.

rected toward health without some dramatic changes. When a church comes to this point of realization and is willing to ask for help, NAMB can partner with another church, local association or the state Baptist convention to help restart the church. We call this "Legacy Church Planting" because it gives a dying church the opportunity to live on through a new work that starts in their church building.

This is not an easy step for most churches to take. We require that there first be a viability study to determine the likelihood of success a new work would have. A leadership change is also required, and we ask that the church property be turned over to either the partnering church, local association, state convention, or NAMB until a new work is up and viable.

Even though the legacy church plant is not an easy road, we are seeing more and more successes with this model. Wornall Road Baptist Church in Kansas City is healthy, growing, and has become a vital part of its community after pastor John Mark Clifton arrived to restart a decades-old congregation that dwindled to only a handful of weekly attenders. In New Orleans, a dozen church members in their 70s partnered with church planter James Welch to birth Harbor Community Church from the ashes of their dying church. First Baptist Church in Odessa, Florida, had not seen a baptism in years.

They turned to Idlewild Baptist for help and now their baptismal waters are stirring on a regular basis once again.

If we don't step in to help these dying churches, over the next few decades we will see thousands of properties worth millions of dollars slip through the hands of Southern Baptists. They will become cafes and office space or just abandoned buildings gathering dust. My hope is that more churches and more pastors will focus outward once again and reach out for help in returning their church to health. And I pray that those who need to make the decision to become a legacy church plant will see how they can pass the spiritual baton and see God work powerfully through their churches again.

CHAPTER 3

THE REVITALIZER:

Who You Must Be

DAN DUMAS

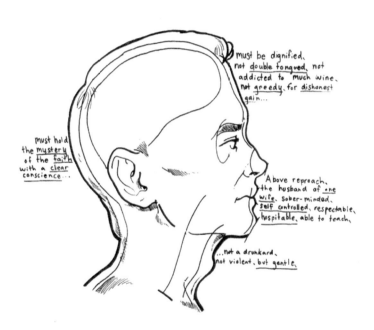

must be dignified, not double tongued, not addicted to much wine, not greedy for dishonest gain...

must hold the mystery of the faith with a clear conscience...

Above reproach, the husband of one wife, sober-minded, self controlled, respectable, hospitable, able to teach.

...not a drunkard, not violent, but gentle.

Being a leader always sounds appealing. It means you get to make decisions, you get to cast vision, people look to you for insight, and they expect you to take them somewhere. You get a serious say in how things go. Sounds exciting, right?

Well, the Bible presents the leader's responsibility in ways that should temper your excitement. For one thing, God is less concerned with what you know as leader, or even with what you do as a leader, because he's primarily concerned with who you are as a leader. The character of the one leading God's people is most vital, and that's true whether you're planting a church, replanting, or in an established body.

Why does God care so much about the character of church leaders? God demands holiness from all of his people, and rarely do people rise above their leaders; as the leaders go, so go the people.

Jeremiah records a rebuke of Israel's spiritual leaders, where the Lord pronounces, "Woe to the shepherds who destroy and scatter the sheep of my pasture" (Jer 23:1). Leaders will give account before God for their stewardship of those under their care (Heb 13:17). That's the kind of verse that should keep pastors up at night.

The good of those under authority depends on the faithfulness of those in authority. If leaders are unfaithful in their lives and ministry, their people suffer.

A Noble Office

So, as a pastor-elder-shepherd-revitalizer of God's people, who must you be? Paul gives a list of qualifications for church eldership in 1 Timothy 3, and almost all of the qualifications have to do with a man's character.

The good of those under authority depends on the faithfulness of those in authority.

You can't pretend you don't have weaknesses, but there's a difference between having a bad day and having a bad year.

New Testament scholar D.A. Carson observes, "Elders are not a higher class of Christians. What is required of all believers is peculiarly required of the leaders of believers." In other words, there isn't a higher standard for the character of elders, but there is a higher accountability. The overarching truth is that the noble office of elder demands noble character.

Above Reproach

Paul sums up the quality of a pastor's life with two words: above reproach. This is Paul's way of saying that the elder should have no loop-holes in his character. Being above reproach means you have unimpeachable character, but it doesn't mean you're flawless. You can't pretend you don't have weaknesses, but there's a difference between having a bad day and having a bad year; the elder should live in such a way as to be accusation-free and without any sustained or legitimate pattern of sin.

What does "above reproach" look like? According to 1 Timothy 3:2-7, it looks like this:

Husband of One Wife (v.2)

The first qualification for eldership in the local church is not charisma, not visionary leadership, not captivating oration. The first qualification is faithfulness, and the first place to look for this is a man's marriage. He won't be a faithful elder if he isn't first a faithful husband.

An elder must be enduringly faithful to his wife and have eyes for her alone. If you suffer from "wandering eye syndrome," you need to nip it in the bud. Those kinds of habits can turn into a

one's doctrine and life. In ministry, you need to take seriously not only your doctrine and life, but how it makes an impact on those under your leadership.

The work of revitalization demands sober-minded resolve. You will be called to make difficult decisions, and you need to think sensibly, and with the soldier-like resolve to stand firm on your decisions. Don't make serious decisions rashly or impulsively, but soberly and firmly.

This kind of ministry also takes sober-minded, unflinching endurance. You don't need to go to Boston to run a marathon, just re-plant a church. You've got to commit to the long-term, and fight discouragement. Sober-mindedness will prevent you from being a prisoner of the moment, and will make you a leader with vision.

ministry-destroying monster if left unchecked.

Marital health is particularly important in a revitalization situation, where your home may be the only respite you have. You don't want to have to revitalize your marriage at the same time, so be in constant battle for a thriving marriage.

Sober-Minded (v.2)
Sober-mindedness is a disposition that gives serious attention to

Self-Controlled (v.2)
Self-control is a big deal for Paul. It's the final fruit of the Spirit listed in Galatians 5:22-23. In a culture that celebrates the indulgence of any and all desires, it is imperative that your people see you practice and display self-mastery. This

includes the ability to control your emotions and reactions in the midst of difficult ministry situations. And it requires you to take dominion over distraction and the things that pull you from the ministry God has given you.

Respectable (v.2)

Every man craves respect, whether it's from his wife, his boss, his children, or his dog. Men, spend less time making sure everyone around you gives you the respect you think you deserve and spend more time living a life that demands it. Put order and discipline into your life. Live with such a force of character that even your opponents and enemies respect you.

Hospitable (v.2)

Do people view your home as a refuge? As an elder and pastor, your home should be a place where fellow Christians come and receive refreshment and encouragement. Welcome your people into your home, including those who don't support the change that you represent.

Your home isn't only for Christians, it should be a place where skeptics and sinners come and witness the gospel in action. This doesn't mean your family life is perfect, or your house is a show room, but you're still called to use your home and resources to bless Christians, unbelievers, and strangers (1 Pet 4:9; Heb 13:2).

Able to Teach (v.2)

The ability to articulate Christian doctrine should not be unique to elders. The ability to teach, however, is a unique requirement for elders. The ability to teach isn't even required of deacons. A man of stellar character can be disqualified by an inability to teach. He should not only be able to teach clearly the doctrines of the faith but also defend the church against false teaching (Titus 1:9).

A pastor and revitalizer must be constantly looking for opportunities to teach. They will happen in the pulpit and out, formally and informally. These are opportunities to strengthen the saints and to exemplify a commitment to Scripture. If you're going to bring change to a church, you've got to make your love for the Bible contagious. Let your people see that your agenda arises from the Bible and not your imagination.

Not a Drunkard (v.3)

It seems obvious, but pastors can't be drunkards. God commands that all Christians "not get drunk with wine ... but be filled with the Spirit" (Eph 5:18). You can't be mastered by both wine and the Spirit, it's one or the other. Remember, your people are looking to you for an example of how to walk in a manner worthy of the gospel.

Not Violent but Gentle (v.3)

As an elder, if you've got a short fuse and your frustration comes with physical manifestations, then you're not qualified to shepherd the flock. When your sheep bite — and in a revitalizing context, they will bite — you can't bite back. Instead, you need to grow in gentleness and learn what it means to be quick to forgive.

Your gentleness needs to be visible in your instruction of others. Model yourself after Paul, who entreated the Corinthians "by the meekness and gentleness of Christ," (2 Cor 10:1), and who told Timothy to correct his opponents "with gentleness" (2 Tim 2:25).

Gentleness also needs to be visible when you receive criticism. Do you become defensive when you receive criticism, or do you respond with humility?

Not Quarrelsome (v.3)

Elders are called to refute false teachers, but they are not called to go around looking for a fight. Do you love to argue? Do you love to be right? Do you love to argue until everyone thinks you're right? If so, then marvel at the Lord Jesus, who never engaged in debate for the sake of debating or belittling others. He only ever opened his mouth for the purpose of teaching, leading, and shepherding.

Seek to be strong in grace in your speech and conduct as you lead your church in revitalization. If you won't lead graciously through change, don't expect people to follow graciously.

Not a Lover of Money (v.3)

Some people think that being in ministry, with the simple lifestyle that often comes with it, will ren-

> You better know
> where your
> weaknesses
> lie because
> the devil most
> certainly does.

der a love of money irrelevant. But that's not so. You can simultaneously be poor and greedy.

If you struggle with greed, you need to give more. The best way to stop loving money is to attack it with generosity. Your money is not your own. You can't call your people to lay up treasures in heaven while you're anxious about building and protecting yours on earth.

Managing His Own Household (v.4)

The qualification that an elder manage his household well is crucial. There is no better way to examine a man's leadership qualities and evaluate the long-term results of his leadership than to enter his home. The home is a microcosm of the church, and if you can't pastor the peo-

ple in your home, you won't be able to pastor the people in your church. If your wife is hesitant about your fitness for ministry then you should be, too. If you "succeed" at church but fail at home, then you fail. Period. Your kids don't need to be perfect, and your home doesn't need to be spotless, but your spiritual leadership must be clear.

Not a Novice (v.6)

The elder is called to exposit and apply the Scriptures to the lives of his people, and the ability to do that develops and deepens with time and practice. The longer a man walks with God and trusts him through trials, the more apt that man will be to speak truth into people's lives. It takes time for trials to result in a genuine tested faith (1 Pet 1:6-7).

If someone is a new Christian or an immature Christian, he is unfit to be an elder. When a new believer is thrust into a place of leadership, a train wreck is sure to follow. With premature leadership comes conceit, and with conceited leadership comes wounded people, and with wounded people comes a damaged gospel witness.

Well Thought of by Outsiders (v.7)

The list of qualifications began with the call to be above reproach, and like a bookend, it ends with a call to be above reproach to those outside the church. An elder must have good rapport with unbelievers in the community. If you don't live that way, you're leading yourself into a snare of the devil (1 Tim 3:7).

If you plan to be well thought of by outsiders, your life needs to match your role as an elder. That doesn't mean you don't mess up, but it means you keep short sin accounts and fight against temptation. You better know where your weaknesses lie because the devil most certainly does. Keep close watch on and attack those weaknesses. If you don't, those little inconsistencies will become chains that bind you and may eventually dis–qualify you.

Conclusion

If you're laboring to revitalize a dying church, you are hunted. You are a target for slander, scandal, and Satan, and being on the frontlines of difficult ministry guarantees you will get blood on your uniform. So walk carefully, and seek to live a life above reproach, a life worth imitating. Be immovable, and know that your labor in the Lord is not in vain.

CHAPTER 4

CLEAR THE RUNWAY:

Preparing Your Church For Revitalization

BRIAN CROFT

It was a cold Wednesday evening when I walked into this struggling church. A young, eager pastor greeted me at the door of the meeting room and introduced me to the committee. They were a friendly group, but timid. Most were older pillars of the church. All were white. The committee had formed because the church realized that something was not right. They needed a change, but weren't sure what that was. They knew the church was broken, but didn't know how to fix it. I had been invited to this first of what would be numerous meetings of a church revitalization committee. My role was to help prepare them to walk through whatever revitalization would look like for them.

The first thing this group needed to do was honestly assess where the church was in its current state. Not what it once was, not what they wished it was, but a realistic and accurate appraisal of where the church was right then and how it got there. I presented five areas to help them think clearly through the process of evaluation. Evaluating these five areas

are crucial to every congregation if it is to navigate the revitalization process well.

Authority

The first question I asked in that committee meeting was, "Who's in charge?" Let me be clear on what I am asking. I am not asking who the bylaws say is in charge. I am not asking who moderates the business meetings or leads the deacons meetings. I am asking, "Who has the greatest influence in the church?" To whom do church members go when decisions need to be made? To whom do church members listen the most? Just because a pastor gets paid a full-time salary and preaches every week doesn't make him the man in charge. You must determine where the authority in the church really lies. Only then can you compare your answer to Scripture's answer.

The Bible is clear about who is in charge: Jesus Christ. Scripture calls him the chief shepherd (1 Pet 5:4). His authority is mediated to us through his Word. If a church willingly submits to the authority of Christ, there is no

The biblical answer to the question, "To whom am I accountable?" is Jesus Christ through the church under the authority of his Word.

confusion about where the final word lies. Once during a deacons' meeting, I had to confront a deacon about non-attendance at church. When he pointedly asked me where in the Bible it says we have to be at church, I replied: "Hebrews 10:25, 'Not neglecting to meet together, as is the habit of some.'" That ended the discussion. Only a church's commitment to the authority of Christ has the power to do that.

Leadership

The question tied to this area asks, "Whom do I follow?" It is essential to identify the leaders in the church. Southern Baptist churches have experienced an epidemic of short pastorates. One consequence of this tragedy is an environment in which church members have to assume roles of leadership spawned by the vacuum of pastoral leadership when there is no pastor. To be clear, the problem is not with filling roles of leadership during the absence of a pastor, but with what happens to those roles once there is a pastor.

The revolving-door cycle of short-term pastorates creates

a breeding ground in which churches, too frequently burned, come to distrust the pastoral office and allow others to usurp leadership roles. Every church must realistically consider who the church is truly following. Only then can a more biblical paradigm be taught and pursued. That pattern consists of the two biblical offices of the church: pastors and deacons. Faithfulness to the biblical paradigm involves having not only the offices, but a proper understanding of them as well. This means teaching what are the qualifications of pastors and deacons and what are the proper roles of each (1 Tim 3:1-13; 1 Pet 5:1-4; Titus 1:5-9; Heb 13:17).

Membership

The common elephant in the Southern Baptist Church committee room when assessing what's not right in the church is the inflated membership roll compared to the amount of members who actually attend on Sunday. How membership is viewed in a local church can speak volumes about its health. This area revolves around the question, "To whom am I accountable?" Honestly confronting what inflated membership numbers mean is the first step to a patient and thoughtful solution.

The biblical answer to the question, "To whom am I accountable?" is Jesus Christ through the church under the authority of his Word. This is seen in passages such as Matthew 18:15-20, 1 Corinthians 5, and 2 Corinthians 2:6. These passages in particular, and the New Testament in general, teach that being a member of a local church is essential in the life of any Christian. Membership has to matter to the members of a local church. Meaningful membership reminds Christians that walking with Jesus in our daily life must not be done alone. We need each other. We need to be responsible for one another. Membership provides the structure for this community life that is found all throughout the New Testament. A clear understanding of how the members of a church are called to relate to one another is crucial to preparing them to move forward.

Unity

There remains a growing trend, especially in Southern Baptist churches, to perpetuate local churches with only one generation present. On one hand, there exist the old, historical, local churches, but hard times and steady decline have left these once vibrant churches on the edge of closing. These churches typically contain longtime faithful members who are of the older generation.

On the other hand, there is the rapidly growing church planting movement where young, zealous church planters are ready to set the world on fire for Jesus: name a city, study the type of young, unchurched professionals who live there, then set out to plant a church in that city. These churches are frequently multi-cultural, and they are almost always of the younger generation.

In an amazing irony, the most zealous, faithful, and hard-working of those in both the older and younger generations in these churches agree on something: that one of their biggest hindrances in the growth and ministry of the local church is the other generation. Each is convinced they don't need the other. Nothing could be further from the biblical church. A quick glance through Titus 2 reveals the expectation that churches will display a unity across not just generations, but genders, races, and socio-ethnic boundaries as well. True spiritual life will never happen in a

church that narrows its focus to the exclusion of believers who don't "fit the profile." As a result, a very important question to ask in preparation for revitalization is, "Who is my brother?" Regardless of how different he or she is from me, "Will I love this person like he is my brother in Christ?"

Worship

The Bible is clear that Christians are supposed to gather regularly to worship together (Heb 10:25). But a question every church needs to ask, especially as they set their hands to pursue new life as a church, is, "Why do we gather?" Too often, the Lord's Day gathering of the local church becomes a meeting of preferences instead of a time to unite under the power of God's Word for the purpose of worshipping Jesus Christ. Songs and music styles are chosen to meet all the different musical preferences instead of being content-driven and musically simple. Sermons become topics about what people want to hear instead of straightforwardly reading and preaching God's Word as the central focus of the local church when it gathers. While Scripture expects that unbelievers will be present during the church's corporate worship (1 Cor 14:24), corporate worship is not about the unbeliever. It is about bringing glory to God through the proclamation of the gospel and its implications for all of life. The best formula to prepare a church for the Lord's coming is a deep conviction that the power of the Spirit of God operating through the Word of God is what breathes life into any and every church. If a church truly believes that God's Word builds the church, then it must be reflected first and foremost when the church gathers for corporate worship.

Conclusion

Evaluating these five areas is imperative to assessing the health not only of a church in need of revitalization, but any local church. These five areas speak to the core of the church's life and define who a church is and where the church is going. These areas are a tool and nothing more. But they can be an invaluable guide for a church to gain clarity on why something needs to change and what that might be.

CHAPTER 5

LEAD FROM THE FRONT:

The Priority of Expository Preaching

DAVID E. PRINCE

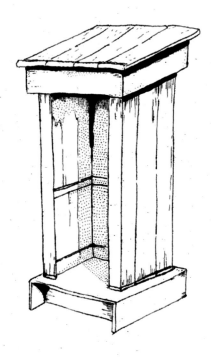

John Broadus began his classic homiletics text *On the Preparation and Delivery of Sermons* explaining the unique and indispensible role of expository preaching in the life of the church:

> When a man who is apt in teaching, whose soul is on fire with the truth which he trusts has saved him and hopes will save others, speaks to his fellow-men, face-to-face, eye-to-eye; and electric sympathies flash to and fro between him and his hearers, till they lift each other up, higher and higher, into the intensest thought, and the most impassioned emotion—higher and yet higher, till they are borne as on chariots of fire above the world, there is a power to move men, to influence character, life, destiny, such as no printed page can ever possess. Pastoral work is of immense importance, and all preachers should be diligent in performing it. But it cannot take the place of preaching, nor fully compensate for lack of power in the pulpit.[1]

Expository Preaching and Revitalization Acts of Spiritual Warfare

While genuine church revitalization certainly involves more than preaching, it can never bypass or minimize the pulpit. Preaching is God's chosen medium, and it will never go out of date. Humanity lives in the context of a battle of sermons. The Bible begins with the divine king of the universe proclaiming his Word, but another voice intruded and clashed. The appearance of the serpent contradicting God's Word with his own proclamation is the first example of spiritual warfare in Scripture. From the creation of the cosmos, kingdom warfare has been a conflict over the Word of God. The entire biblical storyline follows this ongoing cosmic war.

Thus, one uniquely called to preach the Word of God in a local church stands in direct opposition to Satan's parasitic kingdom and at the apex of kingdom conflict in this age. Martin Luther explained the warfare of preaching:

> How difficult an occupation preaching is. Indeed, to preach

> the Word of God is nothing less than to bring upon oneself all the furies of hell and of Satan, and therefore also of ... every power of the world. It is the most dangerous kind of life to throw oneself in the way of Satan's many teeth.[2]

I fear Luther's words sound melodramatic to many contemporary evangelicals who have lost a sense of what is at stake in preaching the Word. It is a hollow victory in evangelicalism to have won the battle for the Bible in the academy only to domesticate it in our pulpits. The only hope of faithfulness in the battle of church revitalization is to understand preaching as a nonnegotiable act of spiritual war.

The greatest need in the church and the world is faithful, Christ-centered, expository preaching. The most powerful weapon in cosmic battle and the primary means of transforming grace is the straightforward, unadulterated proclamation of the Word of Christ. C.H. Spurgeon hauntingly asserted, "The moment the Church of God shall despise the pulpit, God will despise her."[3]

Revitalization Only Comes to Those Who Hear From Christ

James P. Boyce declared, "Faithful preaching constitutes the voice of God — of the living God. It is the invitation of Christ — the ever-present Christ."[4] Listeners are not simply hearing about Christ; they are hearing Christ through his feeble but faithful preachers. Salvation and sanctification come only when his voice is heard, and the listener responds, not to the preacher but to Christ in faith. Paul commends the church in Thessalonica, saying, "when you received the Word of God, which you heard from us, you accepted it not as the word of men but as what it really is, the Word of God" (1 Thess 2:13). To the Corinthian church, Paul states his proclamation among them was "a powerful demonstration by the Spirit" (1 Cor 2:3-4). Every other medium used to convey biblical truth is an impoverished substitute for the vivid, living face-to-faceness of biblical preaching. As D. Martyn Lloyd-Jones wrote, "True preaching, after all, is God acting. It is not

Jesus himself was fundamentally a preacher.

just a man uttering words; it is God using him."[5]

Jesus himself was fundamentally a preacher. Luke records the Galilean crowds pleading with Jesus to stay and continue his ministry of healing and exorcism, to which he responds, "I must preach the good news of the kingdom of God to the other towns as well; for I was sent for this purpose" (Luke 4:43). Later, Jesus tells a parable and asserts that, for those who shut their ears to the voice of God in the Scriptures, "Neither will they be convinced if someone should rise from the dead" (Luke 16:31). It is striking, as Walter Moberly points out, that to convince his disciples that he was alive and that the messianic promise of redemption and kingdom remained, "the risen Jesus offers no new

visions from heaven or mysteries from beyond the grave but instead focuses on patient exposition of Israel's Scripture."[6]

It is possible that minimizing preaching in church revitalization may lead to greater short-term peace and even result in you being declared a creative, innovative leader. If so, you will have received your reward in full. Weak-willed preaching functions as a rhetorical narcotic on behalf of the wisdom of the world. Only a man with a blood-earnest commitment that the word of the cross is the power of God belongs in a pulpit (1 Cor 1:18). But, if you have that commitment, you may come in fear, trembling, and modest speech, but you know that it is God's pleasure "through the folly of what we preach to save those

who believe" (1 Cor 1:21). Church revitalization demands Scripture-saturated gospel-agitators, not caretakers of the congregational status quo.

Maintain Eschatology in the Work of Revitalization

Every person lives out a functional eschatology. We all fit today's decisions into a story that is headed somewhere. Biblical preaching for revitalization confronts rival eschatologies with the story of Jesus in Scripture. Simply passing on information about God abstracted from the biblical storyline that centers on Jesus is inadequate and dangerous because listeners simply incorporate the information into their existing eschatology. All the truths of the Bible fit together in Jesus.

Preachers do not simply echo the story of any culture, but rather proclaim the word that comes from outside of us — the Word of God. Nevertheless, preachers bring that word to bear not abstractly but concretely in a particular locality. As Eugene Peterson has noted, "All theology is rooted in geogra-

phy."[7] To the degree the preacher is faithful, the living God who authored Scripture again speaks his dynamic and living Word in a particular historical situation. As Gregory Edward Reynolds explains in *The Word is Worth a Thousand Pictures*, "The face-to-face presence of the preacher is a reminder of what is coming (Rev 22:4). It is a down payment on eschatological glory."[8]

The entire Bible is rightly recognized as Christian Scripture because every part is organically connected to its *telos* (end, goal) in the eschatological kingdom of Christ. The biblical narrative purposefully directs all divine and human acts toward a cosmic climax in which all things are summed up in Christ. Therefore, expository preaching that treats eschatology simply as a doctrinal category or an addendum to the biblical story fails to adequately acknowledge the entire Bible as Christian Scripture. Jesus is the eschatological king and his people, the church, represent the eschatological kingdom community who heed his voice and eagerly await consummation of his kingdom.

Faithful expository preaching does not excise a passage from the biblical metaplot to stage it for application. The hearer must be taken to the text in its natural habitat, so to speak; the task is not to fit the text to the world of the reader as much as it is to fit the reader to the world of the text. Faithful preaching drags hearers into the amazingly diverse but unified biblical storyline so they can find themselves in Jesus and the story of his kingdom (Col 3:3). In a church that needs revitalization, somewhere along the way, Christ began to be seen as a means rather than an end.

The entire biblical narrative is infused with Christ-centered, gospel-focused eschatological hope. Eschatology is not merely a set of beliefs concerning future events; it is also the attitude and atmosphere aroused by these events in local churches — those on whom the end of the ages has come (1 Cor 10:11). Effective preaching for revitalization conveys this atmosphere of eschatological hope that pervades every text, a hope sourced in the triumph of the gospel of the kingdom of Christ.

[1]John A. Broadus, *On the Preparation and Delivery of Sermons* (New York: A.C. Armstrong & Son, 1887), 17-18.

[2]Martin Luther, *D. Martin Luthers Werke*, Kritische Gesamtausgabe (Weimar: Verlag Hermann Böhlaus Nachfolger, 1902), 25:253.

[3]C. H. Spurgeon, *Autobiography, Volume 1: The Early Years, 1834-1859* (London: Banner of Truth, 1962), v.

[4]"Thus Saith the Lord," in *James Petigru Boyce: Selected Writings*, ed. Timothy George (Nashville: Broadman, 1989), 67.

[5]D. Martyn Lloyd-Jones, *Preaching and Preachers* (Grand Rapids: Zondervan, 1972), 95.

[6]Walter Moberly, *The Bible, Theology, and Faith: A Study of Abraham and Jesus* (Cambridge: Cambridge University Press, 2000), 51.

[7]Eugene Peterson, *Under the Predictable Plant* (Grand Rapids: Eerdmans, 1994), 130.

[8]Gregory E. Reynolds, *The Word Is Worth a Thousand Pictures: Preaching in the Electronic Age* (Eugene, OR: Wipf and Stock, 2001), 338.

CHAPTER 6

RENEW IN THE PEW:

Kindling Congregational Passion for Christ

DONALD S. WHITNEY

Jesus Christ is the glory of the church. He loves the church and died for the church (Acts 20:28; Eph 5:25). Despite all of its spots and wrinkles, he is at work in and through the church. Regardless of how you view the general condition of the church today or the state of the individual churches in your area, the ultimate future of the church is glorious beyond imagination. Therefore, regardless of what your own church's health might convey, the potential for joy is greater in the church than is promised to any other earthly entity. As the local church is still comprised of sinners in a fallen world, there's no denying the reality of failure and discord in the church. But with its faults, there is more to enjoy in the church than the world dreams of because of Christ.

Unfortunately, the church of Jesus Christ is increasingly being viewed as a religious shopping mall. Many who attend do so as religious consumers who feel no more sense of commitment to the church than does a consumer to a mall. As with marketplace consumers to a mall, religious consumers perceive no responsibility to the church except (perhaps) to give money in exchange for services rendered. The problem with this attitude — besides the main problem, that it is contrary to biblical Christianity — is that it is self-defeating. A church that has decreasing numbers of people willing to serve in its ministries will have fewer ministries to offer to consumers.

This is not the case everywhere, of course. The world is well-salted with saints who love the church and are burdened for its renewal. Pastors everywhere are concerned about the increasingly common lack of commitment to the church, not only by nominal Christians but among supposedly mature believers. Faithful church members are discouraged by the new beliefs and practices of their ministers, which are anesthetizing the congregation. I want them to take heart about the future of the church.

Your Role

So how can you be part of the

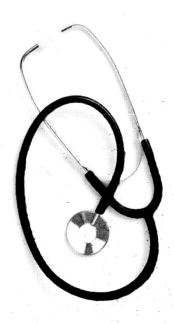

own soul by means of personal spiritual disciplines. But did you know that there are spiritual disciplines that can only happen with God's people? The Bible makes clear that the Christian life cannot be lived alone.

There is much current interest in spirituality and the spiritual disciplines, but it too often manifests itself in a privatized Christianity. Spirituality is seldom considered in a context of the church body. But the personal spiritual disciplines are not intended to make us spiritually self-absorbed evangelical monks. The church is a community in which Christians are to live and experience much of their Christianity. Too many believers isolate themselves from life with the family of God, deceived by the notion that "me and Jesus" are all they need in order to be all that God wants them to become and to savor all he has for them. Such individualization of the faith hurts the church. What too few see is that anything that hurts the church eventually hurts them as individual Christians.

bright future in your church, and what role can you play? If Jesus Christ died for the church, then it's worth our time to find out what our responsibility is to the church.

Whether you're a pastor or a church member, there are a number of things you can do to contribute to the health of your church. Part of that includes tending to the health of your

So, where do we go from here?

The spiritual disciplines are those practices found in Scripture that promote spiritual growth among believers in the gospel of Jesus Christ. They are the habits of devotion and experiential Christianity that have been practiced by the people of God since biblical times. The disciplines could be described in several ways.

(Inter)Personal Spiritual Disciplines

First, the Bible prescribes both personal and interpersonal spiritual disciplines. While some disciplines are practiced alone, some are to be practiced with others. The former are personal spiritual disciplines and the latter are interpersonal spiritual disciplines. For example, Christians should read and study the Word of God on their own (personal spiritual disciplines), but they should also hear the Bible read and study it with the church (interpersonal spiritual disciplines). Christians should worship God privately, but they should also worship him publicly with his people. Some spiritual disciplines are by

nature practiced alone, such as journaling, solitude, and fasting (though individuals sometimes fast in conjunction with a congregational fast). Other disciplines are by nature congregational, such as fellowship, hearing God's Word preached, and participation in the Lord's Supper — all of which require the presence of people.

Both the personal and interpersonal disciplines are means of blessings for followers of Jesus and a part of growth in godliness, for the Bible teaches both. Moreover, Jesus practiced both,

They are the habits of devotion and experiential Christianity that have been practiced by the people of God since biblical times.

Church members who want to see their churches come alive again through revitalization must commit themselves to growing as Christians with other Christians through interpersonal spiritual disciplines.

and becoming like Jesus is the purpose of practicing the disciplines. So, for instance, the Bible tells us on at least four occasions that Jesus got alone to pray (Matt 4:1, 14:23; Mark 1:35; Luke 4:42) thereby practicing personal spiritual disciplines. Conversely, we're told in Luke 4:16, "as was his custom, [Jesus] went to the synagogue on the Sabbath Day," thus engaging in interpersonal spiritual disciplines.

Each of us is perhaps inclined a little more toward disciplines that are practiced individually or toward those that are practiced corporately. Some, for instance, might think they could be all that God wants them to be, even without the local church, just by practicing the personal spiritual disciplines faithfully. Others may be equally deceived into thinking that they'll make sufficient spiritual progress if they are deeply involved in the life of their church, believing that somehow their participation in meaningful church activities will compensate for the lack of a personal devotional life. To lean too far toward our own personal inclination, however, will get us out of balance and deform our pursuit of holiness. Christians are individuals, but we are also part of the body of Christ. We experience God and we grow in his grace through both personal and interpersonal spiritual disciplines.

Renew Together

If a church is going to experience new vibrancy, it can't only come from the leaders and pastors. If it's not happening in the pews now, it probably won't magically start happening later. Church members who want to see their churches come alive again through revitalization must commit themselves to growing as Christians with other Christians through interpersonal spiritual disciplines like these:

1 HEARING THE WORD You can hear preaching outside the church, but we should hear preaching in the church because the Lord does things through the declaration of his Word that he does not ordinarily do through other means. Some of the most powerful and miraculous of the works of God in the world occur through the preaching of his gospel message.

2 CORPORATE WORSHIP When we worship God, there is a real sense in which we are participating in the unseen heavenly worship already occurring. The worship in heaven, both that which is currently in process and that which will continue throughout eternity, is congregational worship. Thus our congregational worship is more like heaven than individual worship.

3 EVANGELISM It brings more glory to God when we bear witness of him together than when we do so individually. In a world where everyone has broken relationships, supernatural unity in a church family bears witness to the power of the gospel in a marvelously God-glorifying manner.

4 SERVING Serving Jesus Christ through serving in his church is an unconcealed way the Lord wants us to express our love for him. Consider the implications of Galatians 6:10: "Therefore, as we have opportunity, let us do good to all, especially to those who are of the household of faith." If when we "do good to all" we are doing good to Christ, then if we love Christ we should especially do good to the household of faith.

5 GIVING The main reason you should give to the church is that you love Jesus Christ and are grateful for what he has done for you. Giving helps fulfill the Great Commission, it's a form of worship, a form of fellowship, a testimony of a changed life, and supports the work of the ministry.

6 FELLOWSHIP Fellowship is the community for which God customized us. Curiously, however, some Christians are tempted to think that they can remain spiritually healthy apart from breathing the fresh air of biblical fellowship. Note the first description of life in the first church: "And they continued steadfastly in the apostles' doctrine and fellowship, in the breaking of bread, and in prayers" (Acts 2:42).

7 PRAYER If congregational or small group prayer isn't part of your Christian life, there's a problem. Praying with the church is what Christians eagerly do when they are full of God. So if we feel no compulsion for intercession with God's people, perhaps that alone should prompt us to pray for God to come among us as he did upon the early church.

As you grow in godliness, your church will grow in godliness. And revitalization happens when godliness abounds. May these interpersonal disciplines spur you and your fellow church members on to love the church more, love one another more, and love God more. May God use your commitment to him and to his people to breathe life into your church anew.

Some of this material was adapted from *Spiritual Disciplines within the Church: Participating Fully in the Body of Christ* ©Copyright 1996 by Donald S. Whitney. Published by Moody Publishers, Chicago, IL. Used by permission of the publisher. All rights reserved.

CHAPTER 7

A ROAD MAP TO REVITALIZATION:

Pursuing Faithfulness and Survival

BRIAN CROFT WITH TIM BEOUGHER

When you plan a vacation, there is so much to do. There are clothes to pack, laundry to wash, money to save, lodging to book, transportation to decide, snacks to buy, and on and on. It can be especially exhausting if you have children, but it all works to the end goal of going on vacation.

There has been plenty said already about the key components to revitalization. Leadership, preaching, membership, and preparing your church for change all need to be considered before moving forward in the work of revitalization. But at some point, the work must begin, and knowing the way to proceed is essential. The most well-planned vacation will be a waste if there is no road map to get you to your destination. Likewise, when it comes to church revitalization, a good plan in itself is not enough. You must have a road map to know what to do, where to go, and how to reach your destination.

This chapter seeks to create that road map. But before we dive into the details, it is essential that you believe in the work of revitalization. There is a popular saying among church planters: "It is easier to give birth than to raise the dead," meaning that starting a church is often easier than restarting an existing one. Church revitalization is always difficult, but we must believe that revitalization is possible. We must believe in a God of resurrection power! Further, we must also believe revitalization is worth it. Jesus loves his church. He loves not just healthy, growing churches, but he also loves sick, struggling churches. Jesus loves churches that need revitalization, and we should love what Jesus loves. We must believe that helping a struggling church "recover her first love" is a vital kingdom ministry, but it requires pursuing faithfulness as well as survival.

These two elements — faithfulness and survival — are essential to traversing successfully. There are the things a pastor must do to be faithful to this work, and there are the things a pastor must do to survive in this work. One without the other in the work of revitalization leads to disaster.

This chapter seeks to help pastors embrace both facets and marry them together as he sets his eyes towards the goal of a healthy, faithful, local church that possesses true spiritual life.

Faithfulness

This facet seeks to answer the important question, "What does God instruct us to do?" In other words, how does God's Word inform what this road map should look like? There are five basic principles that every pastor must follow to be faithful, regardless the kind of revitalization work before them.

---

1 TRUST THE WORD It is tempting for many pastors to look to modern gimmicks and pragmatism to bring life to their struggling church. But the answer is the same as it was when Paul instructed Timothy to "preach the Word" (2 Tim 4:2). Only God by his Spirit can breathe life into death. This is captured in the way God's Spirit by the power of his Word

breathed life into the valley of dry bones (Ezek 37). It is the same for the old, historic, established church about to close its doors. Pastors must preach and teach the Word in such a way that they believe it is the only way God can revive a struggling congregation. If a pastor doesn't trust God's Word, he will trust in something else to bring life.

---

2 SHEPHERD SOULS In many cases, the decline and struggle of local churches can be traced to decades of unfaithful shepherds who cared more about numbers, programs, politics, and personal gain than the biblical call for pastors to shepherd the souls of God's people (1 Pet 5:1-4; Heb 13:17). Many churches needing revitalization have hurting, broken, discouraged sheep that need a shepherd to care for them and nurture them back to health. This is where a pastor's time needs to be spent as he seeks to be faithful. If God is going to breathe life into his church, it must come through the revival of his people who are there.

3 LOVE ALL PEOPLE As we see the imperatives for pastors in Scripture to "shepherd the flock" (1 Pet 5:2) and to do so "as those who will give an account" (Heb 13:17), it is important to recognize that pastors don't get to choose who they will answer for in the church. It is tempting to conclude that a pastor will only answer for those who like him and gladly submit to his authority and ministry, but that is not the case. This is why a commitment to love all people in the church is essential to faithfulness. Some in a church are more difficult to love than others, but the key to faithful revitalization is not just pouring into the teachable and supportive, but pursuing those hard to

love and seeking to win those who are cynical toward your ministry. Tell your people and show your people — all of them — that you love them.

4 PRAY HARD The despair and discouragement that often accompany dying churches can create a panicked approach that could lead pastors to act hastily and think they have to solve every problem now. Sometimes the best thing to do to be faithful in a struggling church is to stop and pray and cry out to God for your church and your people. The despair of church revitalization can wire us to try and solve the financial crisis, rather than praying for God to provide. It can cause us to remove leaders quickly instead of praying that God would intervene and mature that leader. If we truly believe that God — and not our clever schemes — is the one who breathes life into a dying church, we better make sure we find ourselves on our knees crying to the Chief Shepherd who loves our church more than we do.

> Faithfulness requires a pastor to love the older in the congregation and realize he needs them in a revitalization work if that church is to reflect God's design.

---

5 CELEBRATE OLDER MEMBERS

If a church has been around for many years, inevitably there are long-term older members still in these churches who long for their church to return to its former glory. These are typically the ones who have kept the struggling church open for many years, but are also the ones who are commonly resistant to needed change. Because of this, these longtime faithful members can appear to be more of a hindrance for renewed life instead of a benefit. Faithfulness in revitalization is to take these long-term members, love and accept them where they are, and find ways to celebrate them.

It is all too common for a young pastor to walk into a church and conclude these older members are the problem and therefore the solution is to run them out. But God reveals his design for the local church to have both old and young in the church (Titus 2:1-8). Faithfulness requires a pastor to love the older in the congregation and realize he needs them in a revitalization work if that church is to reflect God's design. If a pastor will find ways to celebrate these long-term faithful saints that have kept that church going when everyone else bailed out, it will cause them to be most receptive to the younger who also need to come to the church for the church survive into the next generation.

Survival

There are many pastors who have been faithful to walk in

these biblical principles just listed. We wish we could say that faithfulness is enough. Unfortunately, the wounded sheep and lack of general health that accompany many churches in need of revitalization create hostile environments for pastors who seek this work, leaving faithful pastors either fired or fallen into deep despair. Because of this, there is required a divine wisdom and discernment for every pastor who steps into this work. Here are five areas of this required wisdom that are critical to a pastor's survival for both his ministry as well as the preservation of his own soul.

---

1 BE PATIENT In the early years of revitalization, pastors are often convinced they — in contrast to their members who are so resistant to change — are the patient ones. We have both thought this at one time or another in our revitalization efforts in the face of criticism, conflicts, and attacks on our ministries. We as pastors thought we were being more patient and faithful than the church mem-

bers. As the years have passed, we have realized increasingly that it was the other way around; these faithful saints wounded by previous pastors were the patient ones. They were patient with us as we grew as preachers, as we learned to love them, and as we made rookie mistakes. They were patient through all the changes they did not understand or agree with, yet somehow trusted us not knowing how this would turn out. The longer a pastor endures, is patient, and stays, the greater will become his realization that he was shown much grace.

Patience might be the most important key to survival as it will cause a pastor to wait when he needs to wait. It will cause a pastor to make decisions with a longer view in mind. Patience will cause a pastor to forebear with a difficult person. Patience is not just a significant fruit of the Spirit in every Christian's life but a key element to both surviving and avoiding great discouragement. And if that is not persuasive enough, let us be reminded that patience is commanded of the pastor, "I solemnly charge you in the presence of God and of Christ Jesus, who is to judge the living and the dead, and by his appearing and his kingdom: preach the Word; be ready in season and out of season; reprove, rebuke, exhort, with great patience and instruction" (2 Tim 4:1-2).

---

2 **EXPECT SUFFERING** If you are a pastor trying to revitalize a church holding on to the hope suffering will not come, you should find another line of work now. It is amazing the number of pastors ready to resign after about two years of ministry in one place because they finally met the adversaries the enemy placed in an open door of ministry. As many pastors talk through discouragement and struggles, we eventually ask them, "Did you think becoming the pastor of that church would not bring with it adversaries to your gospel ministry?"

Ironically, in many cases it is their confrontation with adversaries against the gospel and their ministries that make them conclude it is time for the next place of ministry. The

Apostle Paul takes the opposite approach — the presence of adversaries makes him conclude he must stay longer: "But I will remain in Ephesus until Pentecost; for a wide door for effective service has opened to me, and there are many adversaries" (1 Cor 16:8-9).

Becoming a pastor means placing our families on the front lines of spiritual battle. Why are pastors so surprised when the enemy comes against our gospel ministry, especially in places it has been suppressed for decades? Charles Simeon said, "Brothers we must not mind a little suffering." Expect suffering in this work of revitalization so when it does come, you will not be shocked, and preparation for this suffering can lead to your survival through it.

---

3 **PICK BATTLES WISELY** A key to a soldier's survival on the battlefield is to know there are land mines out there and to avoid stepping on them. The work of revitalization is similar in that you can survive a long time if you can know where the battles are, and know which ones to fight and when to fight them.

Yet, even when you step on a mine, or choose a battle unwisely, God will use it to give you discernment to know what battles to fight tomorrow. God in his sovereign grace uses the worst moments in our ministries to bring perspective like nothing else once real revitalizing change occurs. Because of the trials we have endured in our churches, we both have a perspective in decision-making that few in our churches now have. This perspective allows a special wisdom and discernment to choose battles wisely.

So when our newest seminary student is really uptight about those eight to 10 members on the fringe or those family members of long-time church members still on the rolls, he does not remember the blood, sweat, tears, and bruises that came to remove hundreds of members a few years ago. He does not know about the finger pointing threat received in the deacons meeting five years earlier. God grows a unique discernment and wisdom in you through the

pastoral scars of battle. Nothing can serve a pastor as well as the wisdom wrought by scars. Those scars will bring wisdom, and that wisdom is a key to survival.

4 LOVE DIFFICULT PEOPLE We all want everyone to receive us and our ministries instantly. But we have learned that it is sweeter and more rewarding to have church members love and trust you who once were hostile to you. We have some incredibly supportive people in our churches now, but the relationships that mean the most are those with whom we fought in the early years, struggled to love in any way, and yet grew and learned to love. To be greeted every Sunday with a smile, hug, and warmth by the man who led the charge to get you fired just a few years ago is hard to describe.

There is a special evidence of God's redemptive grace every time a pastor sees that man in the church who was once his foe, but now is his friend. Without a commitment to love the most difficult of people through the conflicts and struggles, this relationship redemption is not experienced. Loving those who are hostile to you and your ministry is essential to discern whether they are a wolf in sheep's clothing or a hurting sheep longing to trust a shepherd who would prove worthy of that trust. We must not forget that all persons (including us) can be difficult to love at times, as the poem reminds us: "To dwell above with saints we love, that will be grace and glory. But to live below with folks we know, now that's a different story!" Sometimes that is a very different story, but a key part of revitalization is let-

ting Christ love difficult people through you.

---

5 TRUST THE CHIEF SHEPHERD
The Chief Shepherd never abandons his under shepherds. Christ promises never to leave nor forsake his sheep. This is arguably the most important truth we must hold for survival. Jesus is with you! He knows the struggle in your church. He is near and working, even when you do not see it. That is the smiling face behind the frowning providence. He is your shield in that deacons meeting. He is there when you are publically rebuked. He is compassionate when your mistake or failure in a decision harms the church. He is sad when his sheep attack you because they do not understand and are afraid. He is your defender when wolves in the church try to harm the sheep. The Chief Shepherd will never abandon his shepherds. He is with you and doing whatever he must to give you the grace to remain steadfast in this task to care for souls on his behalf until he returns. How could we think Jesus would not fight relentlessly

TRUST

for those who faithfully labor, suffer, and endure to care for his sheep? If a pastor can hang on to this unshakable truth of being in Christ and an under shepherd of the Chief Shepherd, the most brutal church revitalization can be survived and even revived.

Conclusion

There is a call upon every pastor to be faithful, but you will not have the opportunity to be faithful in the work of revitalization without a means of survival. This is the road map to guide you to accomplish both. Does this road map scare you? Are you ready to set out on the journey of this noble work? Our hope is that this guide will not just give you the tools to move forward in your journey, but provide an unmistakable reminder that the Chief Shepherd will always be with you as you travel.

CHAPTER 8

ARE WE THERE YET?

Indicators of Success

ERIC BANCROFT

Are we there yet?" asked Anthony, the exasperated little boy who had enough of being strapped down to his NASA-inspired car seat.

This road trip was a lot longer than he expected. He had been told that, when they arrived, it would prove worth the wait and just as exciting as he hoped, but he was now in doubt. He was only getting glimpses of the journey as he could just barely peek out the window, thanks to a car door that was not designed with little boys' insatiable curiosity of the world in mind. His patience was beginning to run thin as the duration of his waiting approached an eternity.

Anthony's road trip experience is often how many pastors today feel about pastoring their churches. They started on the pastoral journey with the expectation that it would take some time to arrive at their destination, but they believed it would be worth the wait. Eventually, more time has passed than they first expected, and they wonder if they are ever going to get there. Perhaps you have felt this way.

Good news. You are not alone in this godly yearning for God's glory in local churches. Other pastors over the centuries have longed to see their churches grow in godliness and for every Christian under their care to be "mature in Christ" (Col 1:28).

While some church consultants wax eloquently today about the promises of brand marketing, engaging websites, and updated fonts on church documents, I would like to encourage you to strive for something more promising. This is an appetite for the Word, a culture of discipleship, passion for evangelism, and unity within a plurality of leaders. When such features are in place, you can be assured you are arriving at the destination the Lord intended for your church.

Appetite for the Word

Rare is the church that calls a man to come and pastor them without the expectation that he will teach them from the Bible. Candidating conversations can include questions like, "What would you want to teach us from the Bible?" and "What translation do you normally preach from?" Such questions presuppose the man will be teaching from the Bible. The problem, however, comes to many men after they have been installed in their churches and begin to preach week after week. Confusion and frustration begin to be voiced by many congregants who were under the impression that the pastor would reference the Bible as a support but, for the most part, would provide "a word from the Lord for today."

It should be your prayer and committed practice to unfold to the people of God the whole counsel of God. This will demonstrate your constant commitment to the Great Commission, specifically "teaching them to observe all that I have commanded you" (Matt 28:20). The best way to commit to this is through expositional preaching, the kind of preaching where the sermon is closely tethered to the text. While there might be an understandable occasional desire to deliver pastorally informed topical sermons due to something the entire congregation is facing, the majority of

your preaching should be done in an expositional manner. Doing so helps guarantee that your people encounter the whole counsel of God (Acts 20:27), and allows God to speak to his people without

It should be your prayer and committed practice to unfold to the people of God the whole counsel of God.

you continuing to "interrupt" with what you would like to say.

As the years begin to pass by, your church's appetite will be weaned off of cultural commentaries, psychological assessments, and other in–complete offerings and will instead hunger for the Word of God. They will begin to understand that this was what Jesus prayed for them when he said in John 17:17, "Sanctify them in the truth; your word is truth." Their growth as Christians is directly connected to their exposure and obedience to the Word of God.

Something exciting will begin to take place in the rest of the church as a result of this growing appetite. They will want this commitment to the Word of God to inform other areas of ministry offerings. They will look freshly at the VBS curriculum to make sure it is accurate. They will audit their youth pastor's sermons to make sure they're biblically sound. They will ask for their Sunday school classes to consistently complement what they have been taught as a church. Even the books they pass around to each other will start to be replaced with more solid and trusted resources. This appetite for God's Word in every area of the church comes from years of preaching God's Word to God's people.

Culture of Discipleship

"If they knew the truth about me they would never want to talk to me." One of our ladies in our church said this when we were meeting. It had come after a recent sermon when she felt particularly challenged by the implications of the gospel in her life, namely that she could confess her sin to her Christian friends so that they could encourage her, pray for her, and hold her accountable. The problem was she thought they were going to learn something about her that they didn't already know. I assured her they already knew the truth about her — that she was so sinful that it took the Son of God to die on the cross to make payment for her sins. After that reminder, it was just a matter of the details.

When the Word of God is preached, people begin to understand who they are and the hope they can have in Christ. This explains why the Apostle Paul wanted to come to the church in Rome that he might preach to them the gospel (Rom 1:15). The Christians in the church in Rome had already believed the gospel for their conversion, but they needed to continue to hear the gospel for their sanctification.

A local church that is being resuscitated by the Word of God will become more genuinely

will mean an intentional pursuit of older and/or younger saints in order to help each other grow in Christlikeness.

Passion for Evangelism

Do you get the same emails that I do? You know which ones I'm talking about, the emails about the new sermon series that other churches are using and that has led to thousands of decisions for Christ. If only it were that simple. If only these "magic beans" produced such amazing and promising results. But often this is not the case. Instead, pastoring your people to evangelize consistently and faithfully takes a lot of work and is done as much on your knees in prayer as it is standing in the pulpit. While churches should be faithful to proclaim the gospel to non-Christians who visit local churches, it is the pastor's job "to equip the saints for the work of ministry, for building up the body of Christ" (Eph 4:12).

relational. While people might have been sharing recipes and talking sports scores for years, it is likely that they have been only an inch deep in vulnerable conversation. Your goal in pastoring is to see a culture of discipleship where people who have been washed by the Word and had their minds renewed by Scripture are increasingly seeking each other to enjoy the relationships God has given them, both old and new alike. For some this will mean starting to practice hospitality. For others it will mean transparent discussions in their small group gatherings. And yet for others it

Getting Christians to acknowledge they should evangelize is like getting children to admit they should eat their vegetables. They might nod their head in agreement but they no more enjoy it or intend to do it than before you talked to them about it. There are many reasons this is the case. These range from fear, to inexperience, to hypocritical lives being practiced outside the pastor's sight. Your goal is for your people to respond to the gospel in their lives so overwhelmingly and so convincingly that they can no longer be silent. This takes time. They will need to see this and hear about this in your life. They will need your encouragement even when their efforts are sorely lacking or misguided.

In time, though, as God chooses to bless his people, they will love proclaiming the excellencies of God found in Jesus Christ (Phil 3:8). Signs of this in your church include a shift from individuals expecting the church to evangelize for them to individuals doing the evangelizing themselves; a desire to increase funding for evangelism efforts local, national, and global; and testimonies of how God opened their mouth and made it clear how they should speak the truth to others (Col 4:3-4).

Unity of a Plurality of Leaders

I don't know what kind of leadership structure you have in your church. It is likely that you have either deacons or elders. I am personally convinced that the Bible teaches that each local church should be led by a plurality of elders. Saving that lesson for another time, let me say that even if you have deacons, this goal of a plurality of leaders operating in unity should not be lost on you.

As a pastor, you want to raise up other men who are convinced of the truth as seen in Scripture. This ensures that there is more than your voice heralding the hope that God's Word gives for his people. This helps protect against your people thinking your pastoral initiatives (modeling expositional preaching, instigating relational pursuits, equipping others for evangelism, etc.) are just your "thing." Those

Unity in any local church starts with its leadership.

who have been around the church long enough have heard motivational messages calling people to everything from giving more money to joining the church's softball team. It is likely that your appeals will be lost on some. But a shared belief among the leaders helps thwart this obstacle.

Unity can seem like an illusory goal in any church, especially if there's a painful history of splits or other similar divisions. But unity can and should be seen in every local church. In fact, Jesus even prays for this in John 17:21, "that they may all be one, just as you, Father, are in me, and I in you, that they also may be in us." Why does he pray this? "So that the world may believe that you have sent me." Nothing less than the reputation of Jesus Christ is on the line.

Unity in any local church starts with its leadership. While the men might come from a variety

of backgrounds and have different gifts, they should share a common theology and philosophy of ministry. While the other goals in this chapter have a more public action associated with them, this goal is often happening behind the scenes and starts from the very beginning of your pastorate. It comes through hours of shared conversations, books read and discussed, lessons taught and considered, ministries evaluated and thought through, and people cared for and prayed over together.

Almost There

By no means are these your only goals during your pastorate as you seek to revitalize your local church, but they certainly should be some of your main ones. While we are all tempted as pastors to keep up with other churches, comparing our attendance and our budgets to one another, let us take heart. God has already given us all we need in his Word to pastor his people. Through the power of the Holy Spirit, we have all the resources we need.

But remember this: you cannot do this by your strength. Don't trust in your formal theological

Call out to God
and ask him
to bless your
labors. Ask
him to glorify
himself in
your ministry,
that his people
would bring
glory to his Son,
Jesus Christ.

training, years of pastoral experience, network of counselors, or persuasive personality. Start pastoring on your knees. Call out to God and ask him to bless your labors. Ask him to glorify himself in your ministry, that his people would bring glory to his Son, Jesus Christ. When you do this, not only will you enjoy the view along the way but you will enjoy the destination when you arrive. It will have been worth the wait.

CHAPTER 9

THE REVITALIZATION OF CAPITOL HILL BAPTIST CHURCH

Washington D.C.

AN INTERVIEW WITH MARK DEVER

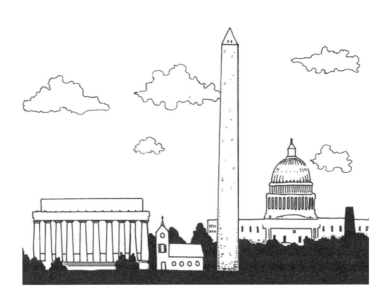

1 CAN YOU GIVE ME A "BEFORE" AND AN "AFTER" PHOTOGRAPH OF CAPITOL HILL BAPTIST CHURCH — A QUICK SNAPSHOT OF WHEN YOU ARRIVED AND OF NOW? In 1993, the church was largely elderly. The building was in disrepair. But the people were faithful. They loved the Lord, though I wouldn't say they'd been well taught. They'd had a long series of short-lived pastors.

The congregation had ad–hered around cultural things more than anything else: meals, certain kinds of music, pro-grams, activities.

2 AT THIS POINT, HOW MANY PEOPLE ATTENDED REGU-LARLY? About 130, most of them between 70-75 years old.

3 WHAT DOES CHBC LOOK LIKE NOW? Now, the congregation lives not in the suburbs but here on the Hill, where the church is located. The last time we had somebody count, 55 percent of our members lived within one mile of the building. When I came here, very few people lived within one mile; even most of the pastors before me lived out in a parson-age somewhere in Virginia.

The congregation is also a lot younger. The average age is now probably 30, and we have roughly 1,000 people on Sun-day morning — so the building is full.

4 EVANGELISM AND MIS-SIONS? HAVE THOSE THINGS CHANGED? With evangelism, it's much of the same. We no lon-ger have an altar call, but in my sermons I call on people to repent and believe as much as any preacher they've had.

When I came here, the church had an "event" culture. They would invite people to church through advertising — the radio, the newspaper — or they'd host a big event to get people to come so that the paid professional dude would tell them the gospel.

But what I've tried to do — through prayer, love, and some guilt — is to encourage people to realize that they have a respon-sibility to share the gospel. We want them to handle it deftly in conversation. So the gospel comes out more easily, more naturally.

Regarding missions, we support fewer couples but with more money. We don't want missionaries to spend the majority of their time raising support. If we're confident in them, instead of giving them $500 a year we will give them $35,000 or $70,000 a year. This frees them up to be missionaries, and it clarifies the relationship: they are clearly accountable to us, and we are clearly responsible for them.

5 ARE THERE OTHER WAYS YOU CAN DESCRIBE THE CHANGE OF CULTURE BETWEEN THEN AND NOW? I wasn't a part of it before so it's hard for me to say. The congregation I encountered here was very kind, very hospitable in a rural-South kind of way. But now, the kind of hospitality that characterizes our church isn't easily explained by cultural norms. It's deliberate hospitality, often with people with whom you have little in common.

Whereas conversations previously would have likely been concerned with family and football, now I think they would be about the sermons, discipling relationships, evangelism opportunities, struggles with sin, etc.

6 SO, YOU'VE BEEN HERE FOR 21 YEARS. WOULD YOU CALL YOURSELF A "CHURCH REVITALIZER"? I've been called that. I guess I wonder how the language of revitalizing means anything different from what we call pastoring.

Also, I wonder how much our language of "revitalizer" is potentially unhelpful. How much does it presuppose a kind of evident success in our ministry, with little thought of the guy who will be the next pastor of the church.

Certainly, we desire to be revitalizers; we desire for God to revitalize, to revive his church. But to be able to say ahead of time, "I am going to revitalize this church" — well, that's hubris, that's pride.

Some folks have asked me before, "Is the ministry at CHBC replicable?" That's a criticism I've heard from people sometimes: "Mark's a good guy, but he just doesn't realize he's gifted in ministry. He thinks it's because of these nine marks, so he gets all these poor guys excited about them and then nothing happens."

Well, I think I understand at least some of what they are saying. But I also want to make three observations.

First, if I'm giving myself to the ministry of prayer and the Word like the apostles were in Acts 6, then that is certainly replicable. There's no way that would be unique to me or to this place.

Second, the kind of things that we do as a church — our commitments in ministry, our theology, our understanding of church polity and membership — all of that is certainly replicable. There's nothing that says this is the only place those things can work.

But third, if by "replicable" someone means, "If you do these things then this will necessarily happen" — if that's what they mean, then I say, no, nothing is "replicable" in that sense.

That's out of our hands and up to the Holy Spirit. I've never once thought, "We have expositional preaching; therefore, we have a packed church and people are getting saved." I'm not even

tempted to think that because I'm sure there are preachers out there better than me, and their churches aren't packed. It's a blessing of God the Holy Spirit, and our tendency is to want to say, "Look! Do you see this great revival? I'm going to reverse engineer this thing to see how it happened, and then I'm going to come up with extraordinary means so I can enjoy these extraordinary blessings."

Instead, we should focus on the regular, daily, and weekly means of grace: the preaching of God's Word, baptism and the Lord's Supper, being a member of a local church, the fruit of the Spirit. It's these normal things that we are to do that God sometimes blesses in extraordinary measure. So, I think the title "revitalization" can only be said after looking in the rearview mirror to describe what God chooses to do to some churches when they get a new pastor.

---

7 LOOKING IN THE REARVIEW MIRROR, HAS GOD REVITALIZED THIS CHURCH? Certainly in

some ways, but even then I do not want to say that this church was entirely without vitality before I came. They were an evangelical church; they were preaching the gospel. But definitely, by a lot of external means, yes, this church has been revitalized.

But just like Paul writes to the Corinthians, "I planted and Apollos watered, but it's God that gives the growth." So, if you really want to press hard on identifying the revitalizer, that would be God, he was the revitalizer.

I'm very thankful for the Center for Church Revitalization and for NAMB's Legacy Church Plant Division. I'm thankful for all of these new emphases, as they are a way to boost the faithfulness of pastors in challenging circumstances. I'm simply raising some questions about the nomenclature and some of the assumptions behind them.

There's a certain pride that comes with thinking, "I can do it!" — because it takes the Holy Spirit, and you can't schedule the Holy Spirit to save 17 people, let alone 170.

8 AS YOU ASSESSED THE CHURCH UPON ARRIVAL, DID YOU HAVE A STRATEGY FOR HOW YOU BEGAN YOUR WORK?
Preach, pray, work, and stay.

I wanted to preach the Word, to give myself seriously during the week to working on the sermon. I wanted to pray regularly every day, particularly through the membership. I wanted to love people and build personal relationships. I wanted to try to disciple guys.

And last, I wanted to be willing to stay there forever. It takes a long time for a church to become a strong witness. I've got folks who've been here 20 years that express to me their pain over how many friends they've said goodbye to. It's sincere, and I feel for them because I experience the same thing. But I kind of took that as the "sign-up price."

9 YOU SOUND MUCH MORE LIKE A FATHER THAN A BUSINESSMAN. AND SO MUCH CONVERSATION ABOUT CHURCH GROWTH USES METRICS LIKE A

BUSINESSMAN MIGHT. BUT YOU'RE TALKING ABOUT SHEPHERDING A CHILD THROUGH MULTIPLE SEASONS AND STAGES.

The more we reduce ministry to business, the more pastors are convinced to think like CEOs and less like shepherds. They'll think, "I want to play in a bigger league, so I need a bigger platform."

But if you're not thinking like that, if instead you're thinking about your members' sanctification, then your entire approach will be different. You can't turn spiritual growth into metrics very easily. This will inevitably frustrate some people in your church, but the elders need to be the ones to have the maturity to take the long view and realize that God will be the final assessor of all these things.

10 WHAT ARE SOME OF THE EARLY ISSUES YOU FACED THAT BROUGHT CHALLENGES? Because we didn't have a plurality of elders, lots of issues became significant. Any number of challenges became threatening because I

was the only apparent authority, and I didn't feel like that was a healthy situation for the church. I also didn't think it was biblical. So I could name issues, but the issues weren't the point; it was the structure that had left us open to unnecessarily difficult challenges.

11 SO, IF YOU'RE GOING TO GIVE A LIST TO A PASTOR OF A CHURCH THAT NEEDS REVITALIZATION, WHAT'S ON YOUR "MUST-DO" LIST? Preach good sermons, move toward a plurality of qualified elders, and be careful with the church's membership.

12 ARE YOU SAYING THAT FOR THE AMERICAN SITUATION, OR FOR EVERYWHERE? I don't know a culture in which Scripture does not apply. So, yes, every place on the planet.

13 WHAT WERE SOME MISTAKES YOU MADE? I'm sure I didn't always have great judgment on knowing how much any particular challenge would cost. There were lots of things that I thought had one price tag, but in reality had another, usually a much higher one. With a plurality of elders, I likely would have realized that more.

I often say young guys have great acuity and poor depth perception — that was me. I had sharp vision; I could see what was right and wrong, but I had no idea how to get there. Young guys need older guys to help them with this.

---

14 **DO YOU THINK IT TAKES A CERTAIN KIND OF GUY TO DO THIS KIND OF WORK?** It depends on the character of the church. If you have a proclivity to be a bit of a fighter, if you have a lot of hard edges, if your wife would tell me that about you, then it might be better if you plant a church or go to an already healthy church.

Some people are just more doctrinaire. They only have two speeds: right or wrong. But I'm asked questions every week,

and my answer is something like, "Yeah, I don't know" — and I am deeply okay with that. Every time I say that I don't know, I dispel any illusions that I'm God.

---

15 **LAST QUESTION, HOW DOES THIS WORK OF REVITAL- IZATION AFFECT YOUR WIFE AND CHILDREN?** If there are expectations for your wife and kids, then you want them to be as visible as possible, so you can either own them or reject them. Your wife should not feel that she is in a fundamental competition for you with your job, especially if your job is the church. Your church can get another pastor, but your wife can't get another husband — and you need to know that more than she needs to know that. You don't want to have any excuse to alienate her affections for the church.

Husbands need to take the long view. After all, outward success in ministry can be more difficult for your family than outward failure because you will have a growing number of apparent good things that could take up your time.

Families rarely work that way. Sure, they can flourish and be successful, but generally, growth accompanies a lot of struggle. The victories aren't as quick, so the temptation for any man is to say, "I'm going back to where I see this kind of output, as opposed to here where I just feel taken for granted and where nothing really works like I want it to."

Success in revitalization can be an unusually powerful trap.

After all, outward success in ministry can be more difficult for your family than outward failure because you will have a growing number of apparent good things that could take up your time.

CHAPTER 10

THE REVITALIZATION OF AUBURNDALE BAPTIST CHURCH

Louisville, Kentucky

AN INTERVIEW WITH BRIAN CROFT

When I first shared the story of my first ten years in church revitalization, I found it to be unexpectedly difficult. I relived some very painful memories, reminders of bad decisions with many unpleasant consequences, not least of which is the still-palpable toll they took on my family. As painful as these recollections may be, I feel compelled to share them in the hope they encourage struggling pastors to remain steadfast in the trenches, and to trust that God is at work in their ministries.

1 EXPLAIN THE HISTORY OF THE CHURCH YOU PASTOR AND THE STATE OF THE CHURCH WHEN YOU ARRIVED? I came to Auburndale Baptist Church in September 2003, knowing this church had a reputation of chewing up and spitting out its pastors. The "glory days" were in the 1950s and 1960s when almost 1,000 people attended Sunday morning services. Since then, this church had been in decline for over three decades with pastors staying between one to three years on average, four years being the longest stay since 1972. I arrived at the very bottom of a 35-year decline, with 30 tired, discouraged, elderly members remaining.

2 AS YOU ASSESSED THE CHURCH UPON ARRIVAL, DID YOU HAVE A STRATEGY FOR HOW TO BEGIN YOUR WORK? IF SO, WHAT WAS IT? I had very wise mentors who taught me well, and I came to Auburndale with two commitments that I learned from them. First, I must faithfully preach the Word, sacrificially love the people, and do not change anything for awhile. Second, regardless of what happens, stay 10 years. I had come to a deep conviction that the Word of God was enough to breathe life into a church and build it — even an existing church that appeared to have little to no life left in it. One precious gift the Lord gave us was another family, close friends of ours, who came to the church with us. From day one as senior pastor of this struggling church, my friend served as my associate pastor. He said he was coming to get ministry experience as he was considering vocational pastoral ministry. He later admitted he and his wife came to care for us in what they expected to be a rough place.

---

3 WHAT WERE SOME OF THE ISSUES THAT BROUGHT THE EARLY CHALLENGES YOU FACED?

I experienced three different efforts to get me fired in the first five years. The first issue revolved around authority: a staff member had plans to run me off, just as he had with the previous pastor. The second issue was defining church membership. In a Southern Baptist congregational church, there are multiple reasons conflict existed. The third was the ugliest conflict and it had to do with defining leadership: what it meant to be a pastor or deacon and the differences between them. Despite intentionally waiting on the right time to approach these issues, they remained a challenge to address.

---

4 WHEN DID YOU SENSE THE SHIP WAS TURNING? WHAT WAS HAPPENING?

After surviving these three firing efforts and an exodus of 15 percent of the church in one year, I found myself tired, discouraged, and questioning whether I should continue at this church after being there five years. In the kind, mysterious providence of God, when the smoke cleared from these implosions I looked up and saw the ship had started to turn. Almost like clockwork as we entered into the sixth year, significant issues began to change. At the conclusion of the mass exodus, some of the most significant families in our church today showed up in the next year — three of the men now serve as pastors with me.

I made some needed adjustments in my preaching where I became more open, vulnerable, and broken before my people — that has been life-giving to them. We began to reach the community, particularly international refugees living around the church. The horrible reputation that the church carried for the previous 25 years began to change as we reached out to the surrounding community. There are many other things I could share indicating that change was around the corner. However, there were two significant events that took place in the next two years that stand above the others: we defined our leadership and accurately assessed our membership.

5 HOW LONG HAVE YOU BEEN PASTOR? WHAT DOES THE CHURCH LOOK LIKE NOW COMPARED TO WHEN YOU ARRIVED?

As of the date of this interview I have been the senior pastor of Auburndale Baptist Church for almost 12 years. We have grown spiritually and numerically, but remain a size that allows the joy of knowing most of the church on a personal level. The average age of the church is now around 35, but an encouraging generational and ethnic diversity is present. There are many children running around and beloved elderly widows in their 90s. There are white middle-class members as well as African refugees members wondering if they will eat next week. We have trained, affirmed, and sent several families from our church into pastoral ministry and the mission field. There are the same challenges that remain in every church filled with sinners saved by the blood of Christ, but after 12 years, this church looks and functions very differently than it did a decade before.

6 IF YOU HAD TO PICK ONE THING THAT GOD USED THE MOST TO REVITALIZE YOUR CHURCH, WHAT WAS IT?

God used what he uses in every church he desires to breathe life back into: his Word in the power of the Holy Spirit. The regular preaching of God's Word through books of the Bible, week after week, year after year, through the turmoil and conflict, in the midst of struggling to pay our bills — God used that to breathe life back into our church. Herein reveals that which God always uses to give life in a soul as well as his church: the Spirit of God at work in the Word of God.

7 WHAT WERE SOME KEY DECISIONS MADE THAT PROVED TO MAKE A DIFFERENCE?

In light of

the previous question, preaching expository sermons through books of the Bible was an essential decision to allow God's Word to do its work in our church. Deciding early what it meant to be a member of the church and requiring that standard for new members proved to be a massive decision. Moving to a plurality of pastors, taking my children on home visits with church members hostile to me, and continuing to pursue and love those who attacked me were all key decisions that proved to make a huge difference.

8 WHAT WERE SOME MISTAKES YOU MADE AND LESSONS YOU LEARNED? The greatest mistake I made was assuming this church and the people in it were the broken ones. The longer I stayed, the more I realized I was just as broken and in need of Jesus as they were. I thought I was the patient one in the early years, but the longer I stay the more I realized this church was being patient with a young pastor trying to figure out what he was doing. I picked some battles

Herein reveals that which God always uses to give life in a soul as well as his church: the Spirit of God at work in the Word of God.

wisely, but others not so much. I am convinced my wife spared me a few more attempted firings by helping me see certain battles were not worth fighting. I allowed some difficult people to get to me more than they should have. It is hard not to take personal attacks personally, but if we can find a way to love those people through those attacks, there will be a clarity and discernment that exists that is not present without it.

9 HOW DID THIS WORK OF REVITALIZATION AFFECT YOUR WIFE AND CHILDREN? My children were too young to remember the chaos, pain, and hurt of the early years, but my wife remembers it all too well. And it had a tremendous effect on her. By God's grace, there is no bitterness in either of our hearts from those years, but I believe some of the physical struggles and depression my wife later experienced were in part a result of those hard years. It's one thing to be the pastor who is receiving attacks at his church by his church, but it's another thing to be the wife of that pastor. As a result, my wife suffered in significant ways that forever changed us both. It is the grace of God that neither of us battles bitterness, but years came off our life during those hard years we are convinced will never return.

Conclusion

The pain of those early years will never leave my family, but in God's kind providence it makes the fruit of what we see now in our church that much more sweet. Seeing a unity among the races and generations in our church, having a loving relationship with those who once despised me, and experiencing members loving each other and God's Word as it is preached means so much more because of where we started.

CHAPTER 11

THE REVITALIZATION
OF FIRST BAPTIST CHURCH

Durham, North Carolina

AN INTERVIEW WITH ANDREW DAVIS

1 **EXPLAIN THE HISTORY OF THE CHURCH YOU PASTOR AND THE STATE OF THE CHURCH WHEN YOU ARRIVED?** First Baptist Church in Durham, North Carolina, was established in 1845, and was the first church of any kind in Durham. For the first seven decades or so, FBC was the most important church in town, but only mildly evangelical.

From 1973-1977, the senior pastor of FBC was Dick Henderson. He preached strong biblical sermons and had a flourishing ministry among college students. But a faction of lay leaders forced Henderson out of his position as pastor. Many of those same influential businessmen/deacons were still in power when I arrived to pastor. After Henderson left, several other men served as pastor, having similar experiences of behind-the-scenes opposition from this faction. The pastor that preceded me, Allan Moseley, served from 1990-1996, and had an extremely difficult time. But by the grace of God, he was able to keep the church from aligning with the Cooperative Baptist Fellowship, the liberal offshoot of the SBC. The fact that so many members of FBC would have desired such alignment with the CBF shows the theological decay of the church.

The church had an extended search process of almost two years before calling me in August 1998. I would describe FBC as a deeply divided church when I came, though those divisions were painted over by a cultural commitment to civility. Some considered it far more important to maintain peace than to live for the truth. Others were sick of the politics by the powerful faction that continued to run off godly pastors, and were ready to stand in defense of the next faithful pastor the Lord would bring. There were some excellent brothers and sisters in Christ who were doing faithful ministry — evangelism in the community, missions in the Caribbean, prison ministry, etc. But there were also many nominal people who, in the end, proved to have greatly suspect professions of faith in Christ, and who were atheological.

> I trusted in the sufficiency of God's Word and in God raising up other men who could help lead the church toward faithfulness.

I trusted in the sufficiency of God's Word and in God raising up other men who could help lead the church toward faithfulness.

I had little sense of the painful journey ahead, which was a good thing because I probably would have shrunk back if I had known more fully what the revitalization would demand.

---

2 AS YOU ASSESSED THE CHURCH UPON ARRIVAL, DID YOU HAVE A STRATEGY FOR HOW TO BEGIN YOUR WORK? IF SO, WHAT WAS IT? I had no strategy for church revitalization, a term that would have been alien to me at that time, and I would have been surprised that FBC so sorely needed it. My strategy as I began was to preach the Word verse-by-verse, book-by-book, to disciple key leaders, to pray for God's guidance, and to avoid making waves while I gained the trust of the members. I felt myself very much over my head, and truly inexperienced. But

3 WHAT WERE SOME OF THE ISSUES THAT BROUGHT THE EARLY CHALLENGES YOU FACED? Right away, I was confronted with the cultural differences of being a northerner pastoring a southern church. A woman spoke to me the first month about my approach to preaching being very different from what they were accustomed to "here in the south."

Beyond that issue, there was just the strong sense of ownership that certain powerful men had in the church, that FBC was "their church." The deacons saw themselves as a "check and balance" against the senior pastor's power, and they generally sought to run out pastors after a short time — 18 months to three years or so.

4 **WHEN DID YOU SENSE THE SHIP WAS TURNING? WHAT WAS HAPPENING?** The issues came to a head when we sought a change in the bylaws to make clear male leadership in our structure. I did a great deal of teaching on the issue of gender and authority, and I sought to persuade by Scripture key men who were opposing this doctrinal conviction. But the strongest of them were implacable and a showdown was inevitable. They called in many nominal members of the church and they were able to defeat the bylaw change. But by the grace of God, he had raised up some very capable and motivated leaders who yearned for a biblically faithful church. And though we were initially defeated, the godly remnant had far more staying power than the nominal members who just came occasionally.

Furthermore, God was bringing more and more people to join the church because they loved the powerful ministry of the Word of God by many good teachers in the church. They were ready to stand faithfully behind godly leadership and made all the difference in the long run. We had a series of really large new member classes and that changed everything. We voted again a year later and won decisively.

For me personally, I had a sense of peace from Psalm 37 that all I had to do was be patient, not give up, and wait on the Lord while continuing to preach the Word week after week. He changed the church right before our eyes.

5 **HOW LONG HAVE YOU BEEN PASTOR? WHAT DOES THE CHURCH LOOK LIKE NOW COMPARED TO WHEN YOU ARRIVED?** I am halfway through my 17th year at FBC. The church is radically different now than the one I first pastored in 1998. There are a lot more young families, a lot more passionate members with commitment to missions and to expository preaching. The church is 50 percent larger on a Sunday morning, and we have a steady stream of young men being mentored for pastoral ministry, church planting, and missions. We have a lot

> The church is no longer deeply divided but remarkably united around the Word.

have been a combination of the steady ministry of the Word of God coupled with the training, mobilization, and empowering of men to lead as elders alongside the pastor.

more young children. Our worship is contemporary now, with drums and guitars versus choir and pipe organ. We have a solid contingent of godly senior adults who love the Lord and care about the ministry of the Word.

The church is no longer deeply divided but remarkably united around the Word. We have a plurality of elders leading the church rather than committees. Now the church is very united around the godly leadership of the elders. There is far less bickering and no factions.

6 IF YOU HAD TO PICK ONE THING THAT GOD USED THE MOST TO REVITALIZE YOUR CHURCH, WHAT WAS IT? The most significant factors in the revitalization of FBC Durham

7 WHAT WERE SOME KEY DECISIONS MADE THAT PROVED TO MAKE A DIFFERENCE? The decision to reach out to other godly men and women and ask for help in prayer built a core group of highly motivated saints who stood vigorously by my side through the hard times. So also, the commitment to keep preaching the Word line-by-line, chapter-by-chapter, book-by-book, rather than to use the pulpit to address the

strife in the church. This was highly attractive to new members, who then got read into the issues that were threatening my ongoing ministry as pastor, and they were more motivated to protect a good thing. The decision to stand firm on a doctrinal issue and not to resign when my efforts were initially defeated was key as well.

8 **WHAT WERE SOME MISTAKES YOU MADE AND LESSONS LEARNED?** My biggest struggle through it all was to maintain a godly and loving attitude toward people who hated me. I was able by the grace of God to avoid public moments of anger, but I continue to struggle with unforgiveness in some ways, and God continues to work humility in me to shepherd people lovingly who vigorously oppose me. I also feel a need to grow in prayer more and more for the health of the church. We had some amazing prayer times during the era of hostility, but we relaxed after we got through that. I want to return to that type of fervent prayer.

9 **HOW DID THIS WORK OF REVITALIZATION AFFECT YOUR WIFE AND CHILDREN?** It was very stressful for my wife, but God used it to draw us together in prayer. I tried not to burden her with specific details of unkind things that were said or "insider information" on church politics, so she could look people in the face, unaware of sinful things those people had done. But the big picture was plain enough, and Christi was a wonderful helper during that time, providing me with wise counsel and steady prayer support. Our children, for the most part, were unaware of the powerful negativity toward their dad, but now they know most of the story. I think the amazing faithfulness of God in revitalizing FBC Durham has been a great benefit to my family in our walk with God. We realize that nothing is as powerful in the advancement of the gospel as a healthy New Testament church.

RESOURCES

RECOMMENDED READING

The Church: The Gospel Made Visible
BY MARK DEVER

The Conviction to Lead: 25 Principles for Leadership That Matters
BY R. ALBERT MOHLER JR.

The Pastor's Ministry: Biblical Priorities for Faithful Shepherds
BY BRIAN CROFT

Replant: How a Dying Church Can Grow Again
BY MARK DEVINE AND DARRIN PATRICK

Autopsy of a Deceased Church: 12 Ways to Keep Yours Alive
BY THOM S. RAINER

Biblical Eldership: An Urgent Call to Restore Biblical Church Leadership
BY ALEXANDER STRAUCH

On the Preparation and Delivery of Sermons
BY JOHN A. BROADUS

Preaching: A Biblical Theology
BY JASON C. MEYER

Spiritual Disciplines within the Church: Participating Fully in the Body of Christ
BY DONALD S. WHITNEY

Reverberation series
BY JONATHAN LEEMAN

From Embers To A Flame
BY HARRY L. REEDER III AND DAVID SWAVELY

Can These Bones Live: A Practical Guide to Church Revitalization
BY BILL HENARD

Church Planting is for Wimps
BY MIKE MCKINLEY

The Mathena Center for Church Revitalization
aims to train current and future pastors on how best to
serve and lead churches in revitalization.

FROM SOUTHERN SEMINARY

Also in the Guide Book Series from SBTS Press,
available at press.sbts.edu

**A GUIDE TO
EVANGELISM**
(SBTS Press 2013,
$5.99), Dan DeWitt,
Editor

**A GUIDE TO
BIBLICAL
MANHOOD**
(SBTS Press 2011,
$5.99), Randy Stinson
and Dan Dumas

**A GUIDE TO
EXPOSITORY
MINISTRY**
(SBTS Press 2012,
$5.99), Dan Dumas

**A GUIDE TO
ADOPTION AND
ORPHAN CARE**
(SBTS Press 2012,
$5.99), Russell D. Moore,
Editor

PUBLICATIONS FROM SOUTHERN SEMINARY

Southern Seminary Magazine
Towers: A News Publication of The Southern Baptist Theological Seminary
The Southern Baptist Journal of Theology
The Journal of Discipleship and Family Ministry
The Southern Baptist Journal of Missions and Evangelism

**CONNECT WITH
SOUTHERN SEMINARY ONLINE**

News.sbts.edu
Facebook.com/TheSBTS
Twitter.com/SBTS

For more information about Southern Seminary, visit **SBTS.EDU**;
for information about Boyce College, visit **BOYCECOLLEGE.COM**

A GUIDE TO CHURCH REVITALIZAT

CONTRIBUTORS

ERIC BANCROFT has been senior pastor of Castleview Baptist Church in Indianapolis since 2008. He previously served as an associate pastor at Grace Community Church in Los Angeles. He and his wife, Danelle, have three sons.

TIM BEOUGHER is the Billy Graham Professor of Evangelism and Church Growth at The Southern Baptist Theological Seminary and senior pastor of West Broadway Baptist Church in Louisville, Kentucky. He is the author of several books, including *Richard Baxter And Conversion: A Study of Puritan Concept of Becoming Christian.* He and his wife, Sharon, have five children.

BRIAN CROFT has been senior pastor of Auburndale Baptist Church in Louisville, Kentucky, since 2003. He blogs at practicalsheperding. com and has written numerous books including *The Pastor's Ministry: Biblical Priorities for Faithful Shepherds.* He and his wife, Cara, have four children.

ANDREW DAVIS has been senior pastor of First Baptist Church in Durham, North Carolina, since 1998. Prior to coming to Durham, he was a church planter in Japan. He is the author of *An Infinite Journey: Growing Toward Christlikeness.* He and his wife, Christine, have five children.

MARK DEVER has been senior pastor of Capitol Hill Baptist Church in Washington, D.C., since 1994, and has served in vocational ministry since 1985. He is the president of 9Marks, a ministry that seeks to equip church leaders with a vision and resources to build healthy churches. He is author of numerous books, including *The Church: e Gospel Made Visible.* He and his wife, Connie, have two children.

DAN DUMAS is an elder at Crossing Church in Louisville, Kentucky, and the senior vice president of institutional administration at The Southern Baptist Theological Seminary. He is the co-author of *A Guide to Biblical Manhood*. He and his wife, Jane, have two children.

KEVIN EZELL is the president of the North American Mission Board, providing leadership as NAMB works to reach North America through evangelism and church planting. He most recently served as senior pastor of Highview Baptist Church in Louisville, Kentucky. He and his wife, Lynette, have six children.

R. ALBERT MOHLER JR. is president of The Southern Baptist Theological Seminary. He is the author of several books, including *Conviction to Lead: 25 Principles for Leadership That Matters*. Mohler hosts two podcasts, "The Briefing" and "Thinking in Public," and also writes a popular blog with regular commentary on moral, cultural, and theological issues, all of which can be accessed at albertmohler.com. He and his wife, Mary, have two children.

DAVID E. PRINCE has been senior pastor of Ashland Avenue Baptist Church in Lexington, Kentucky, since 2003. He is also assistant professor of Christian preaching at The Southern Baptist Theological Seminary. He blogs at davidprince.com. He and his wife, Judi, have eight children.

DONALD S. WHITNEY is professor of biblical spirituality at The Southern Baptist Theological Seminary. He is the founder and president of The Center for Biblical Spirituality and is the author of *Spiritual Disciplines for the Christian Life*. Whitney has served local churches in pastoral ministry for 24 years. He and his wife, Caffy, have one daughter.

PRODUCTION

MANAGING EDITOR: MATT DAMICO is the pastor of worship at Kenwood Baptist Church in Louisville, Kentucky. He also writes and edits for Southern Seminary and the Council on Biblical Manhood and Womanhood. He earned a Bachelor of Arts in English from the University of Minnesota and a Master of Divinity from Southern Seminary. He is married to Anna, and they are the proud parents of Willa.

ILLUSTRATOR: Brian Ott is a freelance illustrator living and working in Louisville, Kentucky, with his wife, Elizabeth. He is also the pastor of worship arts at Hunsinger Laen Baptist Church. He is blessed to have the opportunity to use his love of music and fine arts for the glory of God.

DESIGNER: JOHN HOLCOMB is a freelance designer. He is also a full-time painter and printmaker. He works from his home studio in Topeka, Kansas, where he lives with his wife, Ali. He graduated with a degree in Graphic Design and Illustration from John Brown University.